The
Cat Lover's
Book of Days

© Elizabeth Blackadder

 TEN SPEED PRESS
BERKELEY, CALIFORNIA

TITLE PAGE:
ELIZABETH BLACKADDER.
Three Cats. 1995.
Pastel Drawing. 17$\frac{1}{4}$ x 20$\frac{1}{2}$ inches.
Copyright © Elizabeth Blackadder.
Photography by Antonia Reeve.
Courtesy of the Artist.

Black Cat silhouettes used throughout, by Rod Thomas Illustration.
Copyright © 1995 by Rod Thomas Illustration. Courtesy of the Artist.

The editors wish to thank Elizabeth Blackadder, Dierdre Guthrie,
Stephen Huneck, and Beth Krommes for their kind contributions
to this book.

Health facts from Catnip®, a monthly newlestter published by
Tufts University School of Veterinary Medicine. Used with permission
of Tufts University School of Veterinary Medicine. Catnip is a registered
trademark of Tufts University and may be used only by permission of
Tufts University.

Ten Speed Press
P.O. Box 7123
Berkeley, California 94707

Distributed in Australia by E.J. Dwyer Pty. Ltd., in Canada by Publishers
Group West, in New Zealand by Tandem Press, in South Africa by Real
Books, in Singapore and Malaysia by Berkeley Books, and in the United
Kingdom and Europe by Airlift Books.

Cover and interior design by Elizabeth Woll.

First Ten Speed printing, 1997.
Separated, printed, and bound in Canada by Friesens, Altona, Manitoba.

1 2 3 4 5 6 7 8 9 0 – 01 00 99 98 97

The
Cat Lover's
Book of Days

January

1

2

3

4

5

6

There are two means of refuge from the miseries of life: music and cats.

—ALBERT SCHWEITZER

SIMON BENING.
January, from the Da Costa Book of Hours.
Flemish (Bruges).
Ca. 1515. M.399
The Pierpont
Morgan Library/
Art Resource, NY.
S003995 M.399, F.2V.
Color Transparency.
Courtesy The Pierpont
Morgan Library,
New York, USA.

January

7

8

9

10

11

Along with other special adaptations, the special reflective layer behind a cat's retina makes its eyes about six times more sensitive to light than a human's.

GWEN JOHN, A.R.A.
Cat.
ca. 1905-8.
Tate Gallery, London,
Great Britain.
Courtesy Tate Gallery,
London/
Art Resource, NY.

12

13

14

15

16

17

Waco Doll Show
10 - 4

*There are no
ordinary cats.*
—COLETTE

18

19

20

Tinkle
Courtesy Shelburne
Museum,
Shelburne, VT.

It is a very
inconvenient
habit of kittens
(Alice had once
made the remark)
that, whatever
you say to them,
they always purr.
　　—LEWIS CARROLL

21

22

23

24

25

26

27

WHAT does your cat really see? She sees fewer colors than you (and less vividly); but she has a wider field of vision and notices movement over both shoulders even as she looks ahead, so she'll notice a small rustle in the leaves (you'll probably miss it completely); and probably sees the pendulum swing on your hall clock over her left shoulder as she gazes out the window.

28

29

30

31

IF you choose to let your cat face the challenges of living outdoors:

1. neuter your cat;
2. fully vaccinate your cat;
3. equip your cat with a breakaway collar and reflective identification tag bearing your address and telephone number;
4. keep your cat in the house at night;
5. check under your car and thump on the hood before starting your engine.

February

1

In ancient Egypt,
cats were pets
but had religious
symbolism as well.
Over time,
Egyptians came
to hold cats in
such high esteem
that killing a cat
was an offense
punishable by
death.

2

3

4

5

Egyptian Sculpture,
Bronze. *Bastet, Patron
Goddess of Bubastis,
as a cat.* 6th BC.
Louvre, Paris.
Courtesy Erich Lessing/
Art Resource, NY.

6

February

7

8

Cats can be cooperative when something feels good, which, to a cat, is the way everything is supposed to feel as much of the time as possible.

— ROGER A. CARAS

9

10

11

12

EDOUARD MANET.
Woman with a Cat
ca. 1882.
Tate Gallery, London,
Great Britain.
Courtesy Tate Gallery,
London/
Art Resource, NY.

13

February

14

15

16

17

Cats are a mysterious kind of folk. There is more passing in their minds than we are aware of.
—Sir Walter Scott

18

19

20

THEOPHILE-ALEXANDRE
STEINLEN.
Recumbent Cat.
Ca. 1898.
Petit Palais, Geneva,
Switzerland.
Courtesy Bridgeman/
Art Resource, NY.

21

22

23

Right: HASKINS QUILT
Courtesy Shelburne
Museum, Shelburne, VT.
Photography by
Ken Burris.

Below: QUILT
Courtesy Shelburne
Museum, Shelburne, VT.

24	*February*
25	*"Letting the cat out of the bag"*
26	**W**HERE did this famous saying come from? Apparently, in days gone by, unscrupulous pig sellers would try to con prospective buyers by popping a cat into a bag containing piglets. The animated activity that ensued was meant to convince buyers that the piglets were "alive and kicking." If the prospective buyer insisted on inspecting the piglets, the wily seller had no choice but "to let the cat out of the bag," or disclose the secret behind his energetic piglets.
27	
28	
29	

RALPH HEDLEY.
*A Cat in the Window of
a Cottage.*
Laing Art Gallery,
Newcastle-upon-Tyne.
Courtesy Bridgeman/
Art Resource, NY.

March

1

2

3

4

*Vast, imperturb-
able, at peace
with his world.
There was no
doubt he was a
cat of enormous
presence.*

—JAMES HERRIOT

NEVER allow your cat to sit in an unscreened open upper-floor window, especially in high-rise apartments. Even the most placid of cats may one day lunge at a passing bird or insect, lose its balance and tumble.

Winslow Homer.
United States, 1836-1920.
View of Paris, (Probably
a study for the painting
*Gargoyles of Notre
Dame*) 1867.
Pen and brown ink,
graphite on brown paper,
$7^3/_{16}$ x $11^1/_8$ inches.
Gift of Charles Savage
Homer, Jr.
Photography by
Ken Pelka.
Courtesy Cooper-Hewitt
National Design Museum,
Smithsonian Institution/
Art Resource, NY.

5

6

7

8

9

10

11

IF you must examine a cat who is in distress and struggling, wrap it in a towel and recruit another adult to hold it.

A CAT'S "righting reflex" is an innate trait that does indeed ensure that a cat will land on its feet. But whether a cat lands safely depends on the distance it falls, how it falls and onto what it falls.

March

Cats are born without sight or hearing. Using cues from its sense of smell alone, a kitten as young as four days old can safely find its way back to its mother if it has strayed a short distance from the nest.

12

13

14

15

16

FRITZ ZUBER-BUHLER.
Kittens.
Gavin Graham Gallery,
London.
Courtesy Bridgeman/
Art Resource, NY.

March

*I love cats
because I enjoy
my home; and
little by little,
they become its
visible soul.*
—Jean Cocteau

17

18

19

20

21

22

23

Cecilia Beaux.
Sita and Sarita.
Musee d'Orsay, Paris.
Courtesy Giraudon/
Art Resource, NY.

GUSTAVE COURBET.
The Studio. 1855.
Musee d'Orsay, Paris.
Courtesy Erich Lessing/
Art Resource, NY.

24

25

26

27

28

29

30

31

F OR many years, cats were thought to see only black and white and shades of gray. Researchers have since shown that cats can be trained with food rewards to distinguish between some colors.

April

*Beware of people
who dislike cats.*

—IRISH PROVERB

1

2

3

4

5

JOHN DUNCAN.
*Baba & Billy (Portrait of
the Artist's Younger
Daughter)*
Courtesy Kirkcaldy
Museum and Art Gallery,
Kirkcaldy, Scotland.
Copyright © Dierdre
Guthrie.

6

ELIZABETH BLACKADDER, R.A.
*Tortoiseshell Cat &
Geraniums.* 1983.
Drawing and watercolor.
Copyright © Elizabeth
Blackadder.
Courtesy of the Artist.

7

8

9

10

11

12

13

14

15

*A cat is a lion in a
jungle of small
bushes.*

—AN INDIAN PROVERB

April

16

_The cat pretends
to sleep that it
may see more
clearly._
—CHATEAUBRIAND

17

18

19

20

21

PIERRE-AUGUSTE RENOIR,
French, 1841-1919.
_Sleeping Girl with
a Cat._ 1880.
Oil on canvas, 47 1/4 x
36 5/16 inches.
© Sterling and Francine
Clark Art Institute,
Williamstown, MA.

22

April

23

24

25

26

27

28

So it is, and such is life. The cat's away, and the mice they play.
—CHARLES DICKENS

29

CORNELIS VISSCHER.
The Netherlands,
1610-1670.
The Big Cat.
Etching with engraving,
7$\frac{1}{8}$ x 8$\frac{5}{8}$ inches.
Purchase in memory of
Mrs. John Innes Kane.
Courtesy Cooper-Hewitt
National Design Museum,
Smithsonian Institution/
Art Resource, NY.

May

1

*If a black cat
makes its home
with you, you will
have good luck.*
—ENGLISH PROVERB

2

3

4

5

FRANK BRAMLEY.
Confidences.
Oil on canvas, 89.5 x
75 cm. Diploma work,
1912.
Copyright © Royal
Academy of Art, London.
Permanent collection.
Photography by
Prudence Cuming
Associates.

6

ANONYMOUS.
Cat and Kittens.
Courtesy Abby Aldrich
Rockefeller Folk Art
Center,
Williamsburg, VA.

7

8

10

11

12

13

Most of the time, cats purr when they are contented. When they're in a stressful situation, however, purring can be reassuring. Kittens and cats have been known to "purr their heads off" on the veterinarian's examination table!

May

14

15

IT is much easier
to raise a cat as
an indoor animal
than to convince
an outdoor cat
to give up its
sporting ways
when you confine
it permanently
indoors.

16

17

18

19

20

EMILY CARR.
Koskimo. 1930.
Watercolor and pencil,
76 x 56.9 cm.
Courtesy Vancouver Art
Gallery, Vancouver, B.C.

May

21

22

With the qualities of cleanliness, discretion, affection, patience, dignity and courage that cats have, how many of us, I ask you, would be capable of being cats?

—FERNAND MERY

23

24

25

26

WILLIAM OWEN, R.A.
Boy and Kitten.
Oil on canvas, 76.2 x
62.2 cm. Diploma work,
1817.
Copyright © Royal
Academy of Art, London.
Permanent collection.
Photography by
Prudence Cuming
Associates.

27

Embroidered Picture;
New York, 1945-47.
Designed and made by
Mariska Karasz,
1898-1960.
Gift of Solveig Cox and
Rosamond Berg.
Courtesy Cooper-Hewitt
National Design Museum,
Smithsonian Institution/
Art Resource, NY.

W HEN persuading your cat to pass up the furniture, durable "scratching posts" can be an effective alternative to the sofa.

28

29

30

31

I F you leave home, cover your enticing "family heirlooms" with plastic or tin foil (cats hate tin foil) or spray the area with something disagreeable like citrus-scented spray (cats also hate citrus).

MARCUS STONE.
Good Friends.
Oil on canvas, 49.5 x
21.6 cm. Diploma work,
1839.
Copyright © Royal
Academy of Art, London.
Permanent collection.
Photography by
Prudence Cuming
Associates.

June

1

2

3

4

5

6

If you can keep your cat indoors—particularly if it's a white cat—between 10 A.M. and 4 P.M. on sunny days, you will reduce the risk of sun damage to its delicate skin.

June

7

8

9

10

11

12

TODAY, the life span of the domestic cat averages about 15 years. Some of the oriental breeds such as Siamese may live even longer.

LESLEY FOTHERBY.
Studies of Soraya.
Signed and inscribed
with title on reverse.
C8245.
Watercolor, 14³/₄ x
20¹/₂ inches.
Courtesy Chris Beetles
Ltd.,
London, England.

13

14

15

16

17

Q:
What is the
difference
between a cat
and a comma?
A:
A cat has claws
at the end of its
paws, and a
comma has its
pause at the end
of a clause.

18

—A CHILDREN'S

RIDDLE, ENGLAND

19

20

21

SAMUEL MILLER, attr.
GIRL IN A GREEN DRESS.
Oil on canvas, c. 1845.
40 $^7/_8$ x 27 $^1/_8$ inches.
Courtesy New York State
Historical Association,
Cooperstown, NY.

June

22

23

24

25

Curiosity killed the cat; Satisfaction brought it back!

—AN ENGLISH

PROVERB

26

27

28

STEPHEN HUNECK.
Cat on a Rug.
Copyright © by Stephen Huneck.
Stephen Huneck Gallery,
Woodstock, VT.
Courtesy of the Artist.

29

30

July

1

2

3

4

5

CECILIA BEAUX.
*Man with the Cat
(Henry Sturgis Drinker).*
1898.
Oil on canvas,
48 x 34⁵/₈ inches.
National Museum of
American Art,
Washington, DC, USA.
Courtesy National
Museum of American
Art, Washington DC/
Art Resource, NY.

6

HIROSHIGE.
Cat Bathing.
Detail from an album.
04.357. Japan, Edo,
Ukiyoe school.
Color and ink on paper,
27.8 x 16.8 x 03.8 cm.
Courtesy of the Freer
Gallery of Art,
Smithsonian Institution,
Washington DC.

7

8

10

11

12

13

Why Do Cats Wash After a Meal?

A CAT once caught a sparrow and was about to eat it when the sparrow said: "No gentleman eats until he has washed his face." The cat was impressed and set down the sparrow so that he could wash, but the sparrow flew away. This annoyed the cat so much that he vowed, as long as he lived, he would eat first and wash afterwards.

—From *The Cat and the Sparrow*
JEAN DE LA FONTAINE

Minnie
Courtesy Shelburne
Museum, Shelburne, VT.

14

15

16

*If man could be
crossed with the
cat, it would
improve man but
deteriorate
the cat.*

—MARK TWAIN

17

18

19

20

July

21

22

23

24

25

WHEN your cat becomes older, continue to enrich its environment with favorite toys, and play with it just as you did when it was a kitten. Your cat will let you know when it wants a rest.

26

27

28

29

30

MANY plants, if chewed on or ingested, are, in varying degrees, poisonous to cats, including the poinsettia, English ivy, Easter lily, tiger lily and philodendron. Oleander and azaleas are especially toxic. If you know or suspect your cat has eaten a poisonous plant, don't delay seeking help (speed saves lives). Identify the plant by name or bring a sample of its leaf or flower to your veterinarian.

ELIZABETH BACKADDER, R.A.
Cat and Strelitzias
Watercolor,
24 x 32 inches.
Private collection, The
Royal Academy of Arts,
London.

31

August

1

IF cats could put it to a vote, I think they would prefer not to travel. Cats are territorial. So they are very comfortable in their home environment.

—DR. FRANKLIN LOEW, *Dean of Tufts University School of Veterinary Medicine*

2

3

4

5

RUPERT BUNNY. Australia (1864-1947). *A Summer Morning.* c. 1908. #666. Oil on canvas, 223 x 180.3 cm. Courtesy Art Gallery of New South Wales, Australia.

6

August

7

8

9

10

PROFESSIONALS
recommend that
an adult cat's diet
contain around
25 to 30 percent
animal protein.

11

12

13

LOUISA MATTHIASDOTTIR.
Cat Among Vegetables.
1984. Oil on canvas,
$12^3/_4$ x $25^1/_4$ inches.
Courtesy Salander
O'Reilly Galleries,
New York.

14

15

16

17

18

19

20

WHEN going on vacation, leaving your cat at home is a viable option only if you can find a responsible pet sitter.

21

22

23

24

HENRI ROUSSEAU.
Portrait of a Woman.
Musee d'Orsay, Paris.
Courtesy Giraudon/
Art Resource, NY.

Francis Ernst Jackson,
A.R.A.
*Study of a Cat:
Dorsal View.*
Pencil and indian ink on
card, 11¹/₂ x 9¹/₂ inches.
Courtesy Royal
Academy of Art, London.
Photography by
Prudence Cuming
Associates.

25

26

27

28

29

30

31

E STIMATES suggest that 30 to 40 percent of pet cats and dogs are chubbier than is healthy for them.

September

1

2

3

4

5

6

APPROXIMATELY 50 percent of American household cats now live exclusively indoors. The most obvious result? Most indoor cats live longer, healthier lives than outdoor cats.

LESLEY FOTHERBY.
Muffin and a Basket of Fruit.
Signed and inscribed with title on reverse.
C8967.
Watercolor, $18^{3}/4$ x $14^{1}/4$ inches.
Courtesy Chris Beetles Ltd.,
London, England.

7

8

V ACCINATION
should be part of a
complete health-
maintenance
program for your
cat that includes a
balanced diet,
regular exercise
and routine
checkups.

9

10

11

12

13

LOUIS WAIN.
The Cats come to School.
Edwardian
Chromolithograph.
Ca. 1910.
Copyright © Lora Verner
Designs,
London, England.

September

THOUGHT for the day: training techniques that work with a dog may fall flat with a cat.

14

15

16

17

18

19

CARL OLAF LARSSON.
*Woman Reclined on
a Bench.*
Louvre, Paris.
Courtesy Giraudon/
Art Resource, NY.

20

21

22

ALEXANDRE GABRIEL
DECAMPS,
French 1803–1860.
Cat, Weasel, and Rabbit,
1836.
Oil on canvas, 9$^9/_{16}$ x
13$^7/_{16}$ inches.
© Sterling and Francine
Clark Art Institute,
Williamstown, MA.

23

24

25

27

28

29

30

PLAY is natural for cats. They enjoy playing for playing's sake, and will not only play with other cats but, when brought up with them, will also play with dogs. If introduced to them at an early age, cats will even play with animals they normally view as prey.

October

It is in their eyes that their magic resides.

—ARTHUR SYMONS

1

2

3

4

5

HENRI DE TOULOUSE-LAUTREC.
May Belfort.
Poster. Free Library of
Philadelphia,
Philadelphia, PA.
Courtesy Scala/
Art Resource, NY.

6

May Belfort

Edw. Ancourt, Paris

JAQUES LEHMANN.
Mother with Kittens.
Galerie George, London.
Courtesy Bridgeman/
Art Resource, NY.

7

8

9

10

11

> *No matter how much cats fight, there always seem to be plenty of kittens.*
> —ABRAHAM LINCOLN

12

13

14

K ITTENS often exhibit behaviors and personality traits of their birth mother, even when they have been raised by a mother other than their own.

October

NEXT time you begin to wonder if "Fluffy" is smarter than "Fido," perhaps you should really be asking if Fluffy is smarter than you are. After all, who has trained whom to bring home the dinner?

15

16

17

18

Cat with Fish in Mouth.
Khaligat, Near Calcutta.
Ca. 1890.
Victoria & Albert
Museum, London.
Courtesy Victoria &
Albert Museum,
London/
Art Resource, NY.

19

There once were two cats of Kilkenny.
Each thought there was one cat too many.
So they quarreled and fit,
They scratched and they bit,
Till, except for their nails
And the tips of their tails,
Instead of two cats, there weren't any.

—A TRADITIONAL IRISH RHYME

20

21

22

EVENTS such as moving to a new home, the death of another household animal or the arrival of a new kitten may trigger combative territorial behavior in a cat.

FRANZ MARC.
Two Cats.
Oeffentliche
Kunstsammlung, Basel,
Switzerland.
Courtesy Bridgeman/
Art Resource, NY.

23

24

October

A strange black cat on your porch brings prosperity.
—SCOTTISH PROVERB

25

26

27

28

29

30

31

CHARLES ROBINSON.
The Black Cats' Chorus.
Book Illustration.
ca. 1905.
Copyright © Lora Verner
Designs,
London, England.

November

1

2

*A cat can be
trusted to purr
when she is
pleased, which is
more than can be
said for human
beings.*

—WILLIAM INGE

3

4

5

6

AUGUSTE RENOIR.
Julie Manet with a Cat.
1887.
Private Collection, Paris.
Courtesy Giraudon/
Art Resource, NY.

November

7

8

9

10

11

Whene'er I felt my towering fancy fail,
I stroked her head, her ears, her tail,
And, as I stroked, improved my dying song
From the sweet notes of her melodious tongue.
Her purrs and mews so evenly kept time,
She purred in metre and she mewed in rhyme.
—JOSEPH GREEN, 18TH CENTURY POET

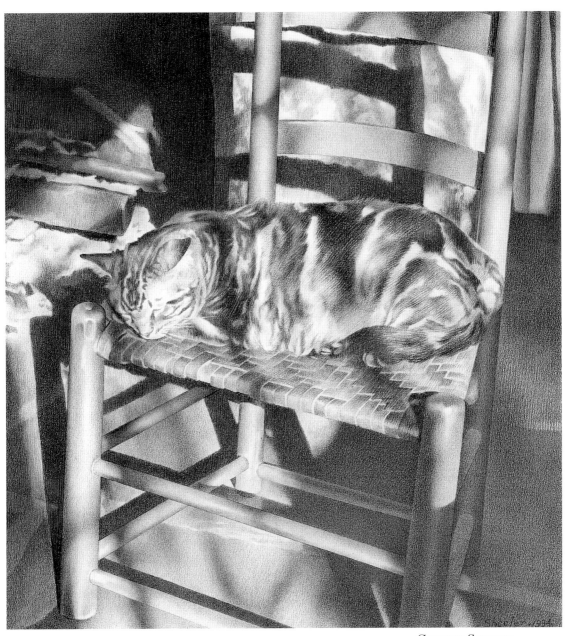

CHARLES SHEELER.
Feline Felicity. 1934.
Drawing, American,
20th c.
Conte Crayon on white
paper, 559 x 457 mm.
1934.182.
Courtesy of the
Fogg Art Museum,
Harvard University
Art Museums,
Louise E. Bettens Fund.

Frank Paton.
Alert.
Bonhams, London.
Courtesy Bridgeman/
Art Resource, NY.

12

13

14

15

16

17

B<small>ECAUSE</small> cats
typically hunt
at dawn or dusk,
their eyes have
become particu-
larly adapted to
dim light.

18

19

20

OTTO VAN VEEN.
*The Artist and
His Family.*
Louvre, Paris.
Courtesy Giraudon/
Art Resource, NY.

21

22

23

24

25

26

27

EXPECTING a houseful of holiday guests? Do your cat a favor and put it in a room removed from the activity with fresh water, food, a litter pan—and most important of all—a "ripe," unwashed T-shirt positively reeking of your odors.

November

28

29

30

A cat sitting with its tail toward the fire is a sign of cold or frosty weather.

—ANONYMOUS,
ENGLAND

Delft Cat Mosaic.
Ca. 16th century.
Courtesy Shelburne
Museum, Shelbrune, VT.

December

1

2

3

T HE tips of a
cat's ears are
particularly
susceptible to
frostbite.

4

5

6

December

7

8

9

The smallest feline is a masterpiece.

—Leonardo da Vinci

10

11

12

13

Fedorico Barocci. *Annunciation.* Palazzo Ducale, Urbino, Italy. Courtesy Scala/ Art Resource, NY.

14

15

16

17

What sort of philosophers are we who know absolutely nothing of the origin and destiny of cats?

—HENRY DAVID
THOREAU

18

19

20

ANONYMOUS.
Mrs. Josiah B. Keylor's Cat.
Courtesy Abby Aldrich Rockefeller Folk Art Center,
Williamsburg, VA.

December

As much as they love to play with them, holiday gift wrappings and decorations (especially tinsel) can be hazardous to cats. Foil and cellophane do not move well through a cat's digestive system and can perforate an intestine.

21

22

23

24

25

26

27

HARPER'S

CHRISTMAS

EDWARD PENFIELD

28

December

29

30

*A cat's a cat
and that's that.*

—ANONYMOUS

FOLK SAYING

31

Veterinarians

PRACTICE NAME
ADDRESS

TELEPHONE
AFTER HOURS PHONE

VETERINARIANS

OFFICE MANAGER
OTHER STAFF

PRACTICE NAME
ADDRESS

TELEPHONE
AFTER HOURS PHONE

VETERINARIANS

OFFICE MANAGER
OTHER STAFF

Boarding Catteries/Pet Sitters/Groomers

NAME

ADDRESS

TELEPHONE

AFTER HOURS PHONE

STAFF

NAME

ADDRESS

TELEPHONE

AFTER HOURS PHONE

STAFF

NAME

ADDRESS

TELEPHONE

AFTER HOURS PHONE

STAFF

NAME

ADDRESS

TELEPHONE

AFTER HOURS PHONE

STAFF

Medical Records

CAT NAME

BIRTH DATE

ADOPTED/PURCHASED

FROM:

DATE:

VACCINATIONS

TYPE:

DATE:

TYPE:

DATE:

TYPE:

DATE:

DATE	PROCEDURE	VETERINARIAN

Medical Records

CAT NAME	
BIRTH DATE	
ADOPTED/PURCHASED	FROM:
	DATE:
VACCINATIONS	TYPE:
	DATE:
	TYPE:
	DATE:
	TYPE:
	DATE:

DATE	PROCEDURE	VETERINARIAN

Medical Records

CAT NAME	
BIRTH DATE	
ADOPTED/PURCHASED	FROM:
	DATE:
VACCINATIONS	TYPE:
	DATE:
	TYPE:
	DATE:
	TYPE:
	DATE:

DATE	PROCEDURE	VETERINARIAN

Medical Records

CAT NAME	
BIRTH DATE	
ADOPTED/PURCHASED	FROM:
	DATE:
VACCINATIONS	TYPE:
	DATE:
	TYPE:
	DATE:
	TYPE:
	DATE:

DATE	PROCEDURE	VETERINARIAN

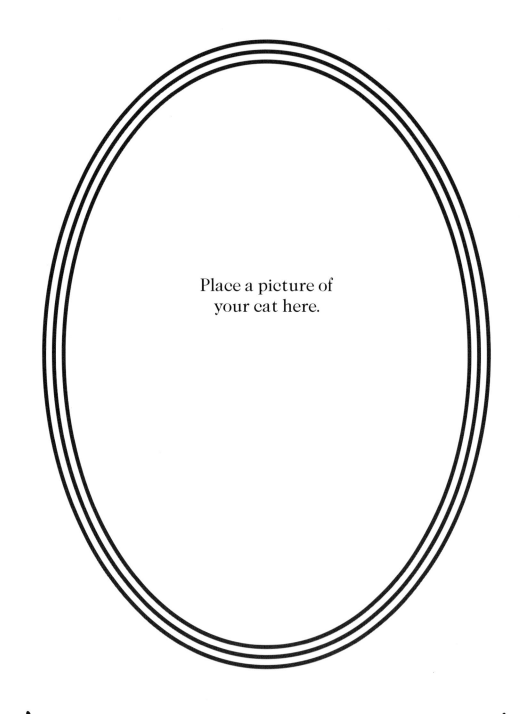

Place a picture of
your cat here.